Ikebana through all seasons

through all seasons
Ikebana

stichting
kunstboek

Introduction Mit Ingelaere-Brandt

By putting emphasis on creating interesting shapes and harmonious colour combinations, Ikebana forces us to dwell on nature. To stand still for a moment and to look at nature from a different mindset. When that moment of stillness comes, we have the chance to marvel on and to embrace the stunning diversity of nature.

Spring, summer, autumn and winter give rise to an array of colours, textures and shapes that is difficult to grasp. It's a show that leaves no one cold.

The variety of the seasons has been a major source of inspiration for artists in all disciplines of art since ancient times and it still is. It is interesting to see how the international Ikebana artists interpret the seasons in different ways, in varying colours, lines and shapes. Nature has its own rhythm and order. The awareness of this is the first step, not only in the practice of Ikebana, but also towards the appreciation of this art.

What sets Ikebana apart from western flower arranging is the fact that withered leaves, flowerless branches, seed pods, and buds are valued as highly as blooming flowers and fresh foliage. The real heart of Ikebana lies in the beauty resulting from colour combinations, natural shapes, graceful lines, and the evocative power latent in the total form of the arrangement. Materials and colours are thoroughly studied before use and are never chosen gratuitously, but decided upon for their physical appearance and above all for their beauty and soul.
Autumn and winter arrangements may not always look as appealing or beautiful to the untrained eye, used to the vivid colours and the symmetry of bountiful western arrangements, but their poetic power surpasses the fleeting impression of these arrangements by far. Ikebana makes us see beyond the apparent reality and opens people up to the magic of the world. It makes us aware that vision is not just what we see, but is what we are capable of uncovering.

Ikebana Today, the first book in this Ikebana series, put the stress on the evolution of shapes and colours in the art of Ikebana. The large-scale Land Art in *Contemporary Ikebana* looked at the interaction between these newfound shapes and colours and nature and now, *Ikebana through all Seasons*, the final book in the Ikebana trilogy shows the evolution of shapes, textures and colours in nature itself. Diversity is what makes this book so unique.

Ikenobō

Ono no Imoko, a priest from the Prince Regent's retinue, decided after three official journeys to the imperial palace in China to retreat from active life. He became in charge of the Buddhist temple Rokkaku-do in Kyoto and settled in a little house named ike-no-bō, or 'cabin by the lake'. Among the things he had learned in China was the art of offering up flowers at religious ceremonies. He started to study the meaning of flowers. This is how the history of Ikebana In Japan began. From then on, many a priest devoted themselves to the art of flower arranging. During the second half of the 15th century Senkei XII lay down the first rules of rikka (first temple arrangement) and he is therefore regarded as the founder of the school of Ikenobō. Autumn 1629 saw the very first Ikenobō exhibition, an event that is still organized every year. Other styles such as nageira, shoka and moribana developed. Imported flowers, make their entry and practical lessons are being taught. Traditional values and principles are still treated with respect and followed, but Ikenobō does open itself for all influences of the modern times. Every style evolves, but sticks to certain rules. Only the free style offers endless possibilities to go from natural to abstract arrangements.

Ohara

The Ohara school was founded by Unshin Ohara. After a thorough study of Ikenobō he decided to develop a very own style, the moribana. This also means the introduction of the kenzan. The import of unknown flowers inspired to create new arrangements. Ohara designs flat dishes, in which different materials are processed. These designs still make the basics of Ohara style. The moribana style was a true revolution in the world of ikebana. Today still, new shapes and styles are being introduced. Emphasis still lays on the natural growth of plants and flowers. Observing nature is of paramount importance, as well as the experience of seasonal difference. The rimpa, based on the art of Korin, are fascinating. Bunjinbana is a very spontaneous arrangement inspired on Chinese vases.

Sōgetsu

This modern Ikebana school has the greatest number of members in the world. The school was founded in 1927 by Sofu Teshigahara. Sofu's sculptures and paintings can be seen in various museums all over the world. Only seven years old, he was introduced in the art of ikebana by his father, who had studied different styles of ikebana. Sofu soon discovered that the art had more possibilities than what had been visible until then. Ikebana has always been placed in a tokonoma. Sofu saw enormous potential in placing it in every interior. He founded his new school: Sōgetsu. In the beginning, he cast off all ikebana rules, though he gradually understood rules were necessary to mould students so that they could be given the freedom that is typical of Sōgetsu. It is very personal work that is well integrated in our modern world.

Ichiyo

The Ichiyo school was founded in 1937 by Meikof Kasuya and his sister Ichiyo. They tried to adapt ikebana to the modern way of living while retaining traditions and inheritances. In 1983, the third son of Meikof Kasuya, Akihiro, became the third Iemoto of the school. In big stage shows he displayed the balance as well as the tension technique. These were breathtaking experiences that inspired his students. He teaches to use mainly natural materials to consider the plant's character, the seasons and the positioning of the arrangement.

The advisory team

Anke Ma-Verhoeven
The Netherlands

Anke started taking Sogetsu lessons with Ies Bal in 1969, shortly after her first visit to an Ikebana exhibition. She obtained the Japanese certificate for teaching Sogetsu Ikebana. To further specialise she took part in classes and workshops with a.o. Georgie Davidson and Birgit Christensen. On het working trips to Japan she took lessons at the Sogetsu school. Her interest in Japanese art and culture grew even more by her travels and contacts in Japan. She just finished a twelve-year period as Branch Director of the Sogetsu Branch Nederland, during which she has realized her task to expand Ikebana. Anke teaches, gives workshops, lectures and demonstrations in the Netherlands and abroad, and organises exhibitions in the Netherlands.

Jeannine Vanhee-Cordeel
Belgium

Jeannine took up Ikebana in the late seventies, first with Miyoko Miyata, then with Birgit Christensen. From 1984 onwards, she set up her own Ikebana studio and gave intensive Sogetsu courses, demonstrations and workshops. She held solo and joint exhibitions, sometimes with organisations as Sogetsu Branch Nederland, Studiegroep Vlaanderen, Studiegroep Azalea and the Hana Chapter of Belgium. Since 1990, Jeannine has visited Japan many times/ There she has deepened her knowledge with masters as Fukushima, Kawana, Samura, Iemoto Hiroshi Teshigahara and Akane Teshigara. In 1999 she participated in the Takashimaya exhibition in the heart of Tokyo. In Flanders she founded the Sogetsu study group and, together with other teachers, the Hana Chapter of Ikebana International. She was awarded by The Sogetsu School in Tokyo in 2003.

Gail Emmons
United States of America

Gail started her floristic journey 30 years ago while living in Hong Kong. She took classes in Sogetsu Ikebana. When she returned to the San Francisco Bay Area she continued her study with her present teacher Soho Sakai. Under Soho's tutelage, Gail recently received the Riji certificate. Gail's trademark in flower arranging has been the development of a dynamic sculptural style that mixes the traditions of both East and West in new and daring ways. She is a member of the Orinda Garden Club. She loves to share her knowledge and passion for flower arranging in numerous demonstrations and workshops. Gail has participated in national and international flower shows both as a flower arranger and as a judge. She has won prestigious international, national, zone and club awards throughout her career.

Lia De Grave-Van Hove

Belgium

Lia took the Japanese degree Shihan at the Sesshu school in Tokyo, under sister Thérèse Yonezawa, the Japanese Carmelite nun who taught Ikebana in Bruges (Belgium). Since 1981, professors in Japan, the Netherlands, France and Austria helped her with Kado and taught her classical as well as modern Ikebana. In 1991 she was granted the permission to found Ikenobo Study group Belgium by Iemoto Sen'ei Ikenobo (45th generation). She also co-founded the Ikebana International Chapter of Belgium. Today Lia is Junkatoku (Senior Professor of Ikebana 4th Grade).

Godelieve Van den heuvel-Janssens

Belgium

To deepen her knowledge of the art Godelieve undertook several study trips to Japan where she took several master classes. She is vice president and founding member of the Ohara Chapter Belgium and Ikebana International Belgium. She organized and participated in a number of expositions both national and international and frequently gives workshops in Japan, France, Belgium and the Netherlands. Godelieve has been an Ikebana teacher since 1979 (Sesshu) and became Ohara Master in 1990.

Mit Ingelaere-Brandt

Belgium

Mit took the first grade in Sogetsu in 1979. From then on she has continued to gain higher grades. She also teaches Kiku school, organizes exhibitions and has been involved with sculpting and painting. These fields strongly influence her work. 1995 saw an inter-artistic project in collaboration with 31 ceramic artists (Argile en fleur). During several years she followed courses and masterclasses with Georgie Davidson (Kiku school), Mit also took several seminars and workshops with Tetsunori Kawana and Land Art artists Helen Escobedo (Mexico) and Bob Verschueren (Belgium). In June 2011 Mit Ingelaere-Brandt will be appointed president of Ikebana International Belgium.

Els Spoelstra-Goos

The Netherlands

In 1978 Els started taking Sogetsu Ikebana lessons with Rita Uilenreef and after training with Birgit Christensen she obtained her teacher's degree in 1988. To specialize further Els took lessons and workshops with Jeannine Vanhee-Cordeel and Marja Vervoort-Biemond. In Japan she followed a number of courses with Hiroshi and Akane Teshigahara Iemoto and other world renown Ikebana teachers such as Shimura, Fukushima, Sumura, Takanaka, Kawana and Nakamura. Els Spoelstra-Goos teaches both in the Netherlands and Finland (Rovaniemi) and gave several solo exposition as well as exhibitions together with Sogetsu Branch Nederland, Studiegroep Vlaanderen and Studiegroep Azalea. Els Spoelstra-Goos is First Grade Ikebana professor and teaches in Belgium and the Netherlands.

Spring signifies the emergence of new life. It's the season everyone longs for, especially after a lengthy and often depressing winter. Bright light, warmth and sunshine lift the spirits and bring zest to life. Forests awaken. The spring months are the blossoming months, bringing rejuvenation and growth. Nothing is as moving as seeing nature revive. From the past, new life is born, at first hesitant and later with full vehemence. Bursting with life, nature is dressed in a bright green gown. We are amazed by the new colours emerging, shoots pushing through the soil, baby leaves unfurling amidst soft catkins. We feel the strong pulse of life, the persistence of hope. Spring is a period of unbridled optimism and joy.

Spring

*Through the bush
The splendour of bluebells
behind an old tree*

Mit Ingelaere-Brandt

| **Hedwigis M. Bogaert-Waterblee** BELGIUM SŌGETSU

| **Jeannine Vanhee-Cordeel** BELGIUM SŌGETSU

Godelieve Van den heuvel-Janssens BELGIUM

SŌGETSU

| **Marcel Vrignaud** FRANCE OHARA

SŌGETSU

| **Atsuko Bersma** BELGIUM SŌGETSU

| **Nicole Kruimel-Rosselle** THE NETHERLANDS

| **Monique van de Ven** THE NETHERLANDS ⓒ SŌGETSU

ITALY **Bologna Study Group** | 57

Everything grows and blossoms, an abundance of strong shapes and colours. In Japan, summer begins in May and is divided into three periods. The first period is temperate with fresh and bright greens. Serenity prevails. The second phase is distinguished by turbulence. Cloudy skies, rain and heavy thunderstorms. An explosion of power and exuberance. In the third period the world slows down under the languishing heat. The fresh green turns darker, flowers and grasses are thriving, but autumn is already in the air.

Summer

River on rock
Applauding the sun
Two dragonflies hover
Lost in love

Peter Flynn

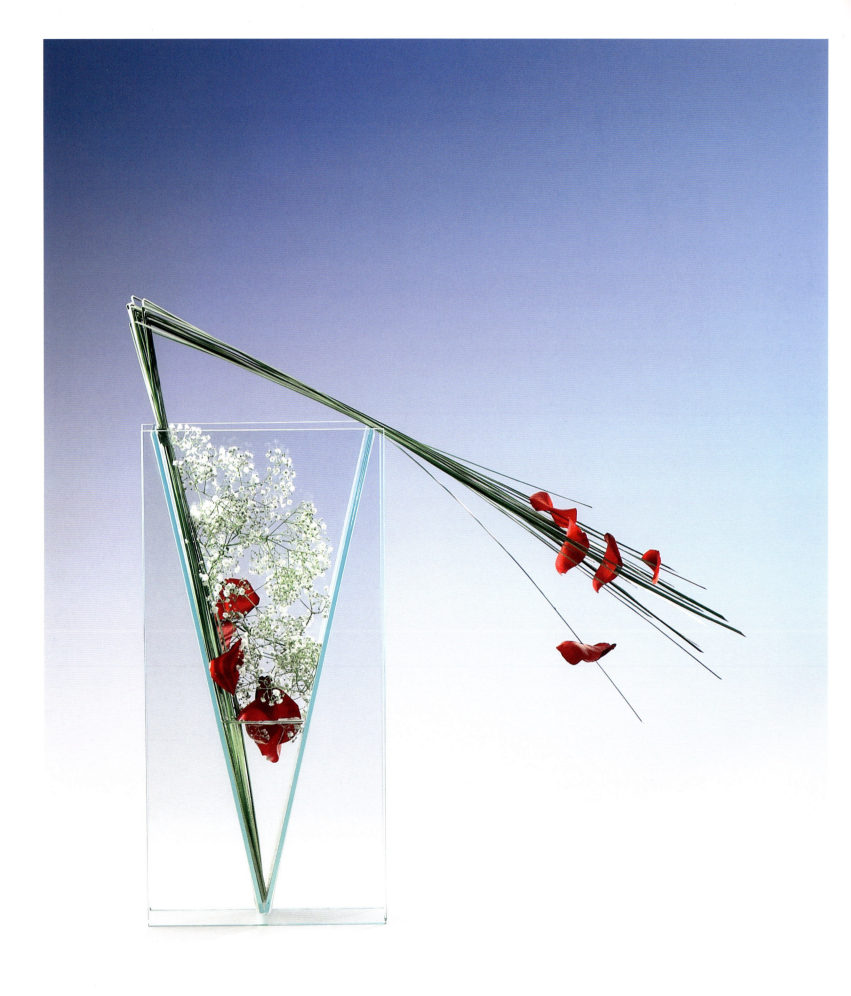

| **Lenie Merts** THE NETHERLANDS SŌGETSU

| **Dominique Coudroy** FRANCE SŌGETSU

SŌGETSU

OHARA

SŌGETSU BELGIUM **Robert Van Hecke** | 85

Autumn is the period for contemplation, a time for looking back and saying goodbye. Colours intensify as if nature wants to show off one last time and end with a grand finale. One last big effort with blushing apples, succulent berries, and leaves in astonishing shades of gold and copper. It is time to harvest and to store the fruits of our labours for enjoyment later. The days are getting shorter and cold air starts to rush in, winter is just behind the corner.

Autumn

Above russet and gold leaves
Starlings
Pebbles flung from
A child's hand

Peter Flynn

SŌGETSU

Godelieve Van den heuvel-Janssens BELGIUM SÔGETSU

SŌGETSU

| **Hedwigis M. Bogaert-Waterblee** BELGIUM SÔGETSU

SŌGETSU

SŌGETSU

| **Christina Lindner** GERMANY SŌGETSU

SŌGETSU

Slumbering, sleeping, dreaming. Colours fade and disappear. Only structures and skeletons remain. Trees and bushes stand naked without their coat of greenery. We discover the power and stubborn will of nature. Holding strong after all warm protection, softness and tenderness have left.

Winter brings snow and white wonderlands. The world is a fairy tale. Covered in a layer of white, the world seems to be shifting. The light changes, sounds are muffled, all is quietly covered under a protective layer of snow. As if nature is debating its next step, softly whispering and contemplating its winning move to overcome the cold and gloom of winter. The fairy tale concludes with a happy end when all of a sudden new, colourful sprouts pop up, full of hope and new energy.

Winter

Near the river
The silence of stones
In the white world

Mit Ingelaere-Brandt

| **Jenneke Soejoko-Oosterveld** THE NETHERLANDS

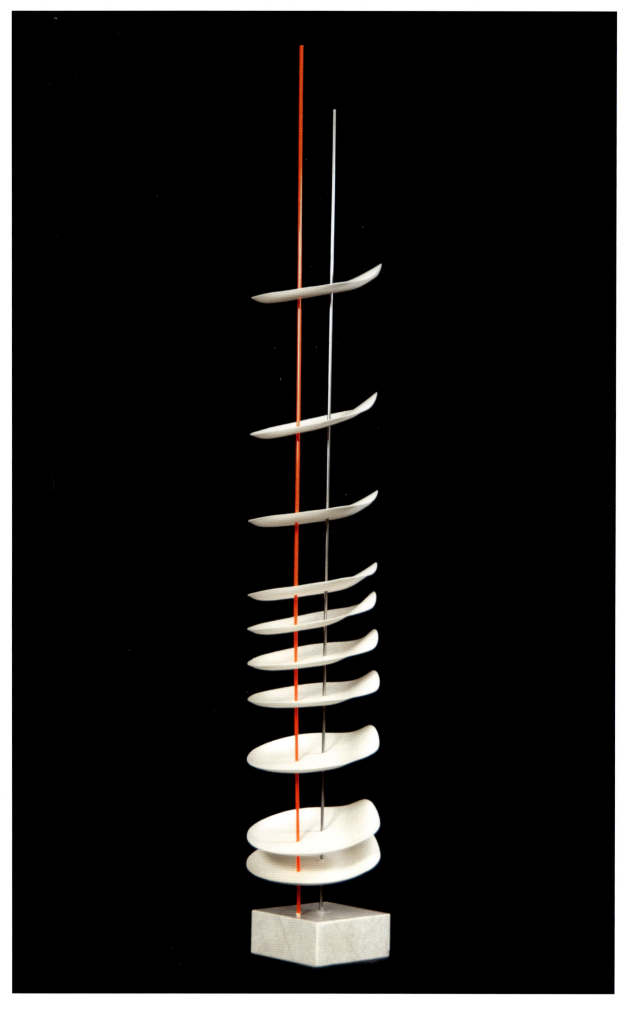

Wil Oortman-de Theye THE NETHERLANDS SŌGETSU

BELGIUM **Mit Ingelaere-Brandt** | 163

SŌGETSU

SŌGETSU

SŌGETSU

| **Tanya Balnaves** AUSTRALIA
SŌGETSU

| **Misha Huurman** THE NETHERLANDS SŌGETSU

SŌGETSU

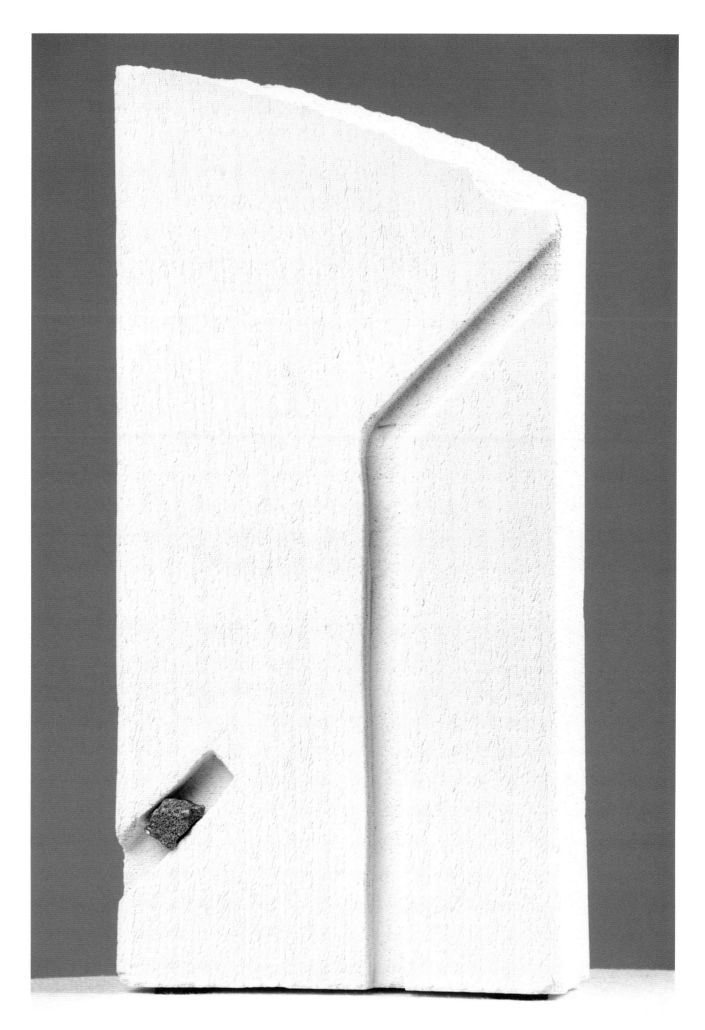

SŌGETSU

Ikebana

the artists

ELIZABETH ANGELL
Australia

 SŌGETSU

Photography:
Benoit Trudeau

p109 > Citrus japonica (kumquat), Corokia cotoneaster, Monstera

TANYA BALNAVES
Australia

 SŌGETSU

Photography:
David Ryan

p178 > Eucalyptus xanthonema, Spaghnum, drift wood

DINI BASTIAANSSEN-ENGELS
The Netherlands

SŌGETSU

Photography:
FJM Bastiaanssen

p69 > Cotinus, Opuntia robusta, Paeonia

ATSUKO BERSMA
Belgium

SŌGETSU

Photography:
Philippe Desnerck

p38 > Euonymus alatus, Eustoma grandiflora
p64 > Rosa, Xanthorrhoea
p107 > Anthurium (dried leaf), Sandersonia aurantiaca
p4, 159 > Zantedeschia

ILSE BEUNEN
Belgium

SŌGETSU

Photography:
Pierre Volpe (Adiffrent View bvba)

p2, 91 > Anthurium, Phormium tenax 'Yellow Wave'
p181 > Cornus alba 'Sibirica', Salix alba

HEDWIGIS M. BOGAERT-WATERBLEE
Belgium

SŌGETSU

Photography:
Daniel Ieper

p13 > Tulipa 'Parrot', Xanthorrhoea **p14 >** Corylus avellana 'Contorta',
Berberis thunbergii 'Sulphureum', Narcissus **p112 >** Cotoneaster conspicuus,
Tilia, Zantedeschia 'Mango' **p170 >** Anthurium x hybrid, Artemisia 'Powis Castle'

ADRIAAN BRAAMSE
The Netherlands

SŌGETSU

Photography:
Fotostudio Zuylenburg

p119 > Beta vulgaris 'Rainbow Chard'

JEAN BROUWERS
The Netherlands

SŌGETSU

Photography:
Fotostudio Zuylenburg

p39 > Acacia
p72 > Hydrangea, Magnolia

MIEKE BRUYNOOGHE-VAN ELSLANDE
Belgium

 SŌGETSU

Photography:
Denise Priem-Willemarck

p142 > Actinidia arguta, Cucurbita, Dianthus barbatus

BRIGITTA BUSE
Germany

SŌGETSU

Photography:
Felix Buse

p188 > Phyllostachys

NELLY CAUTEREELS
Belgium

OHARA

Photography:
Jef Cuylen

p86 > Galium palustre, Hippuris vulgaris, Nymphaea, Pontederia
p153 > Corylus avellana 'Contorta', Gypsophila, Pinus

DOMINIQUE COUDROY
France

SŌGETSU

Photography:
James Aljami (Photo LVR)

p78 > Arum maculatum, Betula pendula, Hyacinthus, Prunus spinosa

FIORELLA FALAVIGNA DE LEO AND BOLOGNA STUDY GROUP
Italy

OHARA

Photography:
Antonella Amatulli

p57 > Prunus avium, Ranunculus asiaticus
p172-173 > Hydrangea macrophylla, Pinus pinea, Wisteria sinensis

ANTOINETTE DE MEY-DE ROO
Belgium

SŌGETSU

Photography:
Denise Priem

p189 > Alchemilla mollis, Zantedeschia

MARIJKE DE RUITER
The Netherlands

SŌGETSU

Photography:
Fotostudio Zuylenburg

p79 > Hydrangea, Wisteria

NICOLE DINEUR
France

SŌGETSU

Photography:
Jean-Pierre Salmon

p47 > Anthurium (leaves), Arum (Calla)

RITA DOLLBERG
Germany

 SŌGETSU

Photography:
Marion Hogl

p118 > Callicarpa japonica, Radicchio di Treviso

GEORGINE DU QUESNE VAN BRUCHEM-MEINERS
France

 ICHIYO

Photography:
N.F. du Quesne van Bruchem

p15 > Dendrobium 'Burana', Prunus dulcis
p117 > Chrysanthemum, Cotinus coggyria, Hippophae rhamnoides, Phyllostachys edulis

GAIL EMMONS
United States

 SŌGETSU

Photography:
George Post

p26 > Agapanthus africans 'Peter Pan' (stems), Aspidistra elatior 'Asahi', Clematis viticella
p96-97 > Acer aceraceae, Punica granatum, dried twisted Wisteria branch
p98 > Celastrus orbiculatus, Cucurbita

AYAKO GRAEFE
Germany

SŌGETSU

Photography:
Helmuth E. Günther

p52-53 > Narcissus, Salix gracilistyla
p136 > Chrysanthemum, Gentiana, Miscanthus sinensis, Rosa canina, Xanthorrhoea
p152 > Aspidistra elatior, Gossypium

BRIGITTE WÖLKER, HAGEN MASSANECK, INGEBORG WALTER, EDELGARD HERWALD, URSULA ERLINGHAGEN
Germany

SŌGETSU
Photography: Hagen Massaneck

p179 > Cotoneaster, Spinifex, wood, veneer

MISHA HUURMAN
The Netherlands

SŌGETSU

Photography:
Fotostudio Zuylenburg

p182-183 > Amaryllis, Calamus rotang

MIT INGELAERE-BRANDT
Belgium

 SŌGETSU

Photography:
Annika Ingelaere

p58-59 > Aspidistra, Azalea, Fargesia   **p93 >** Chaenomeles japonica, Gerbera, Primula   **p144-145 >** Platanus   **p163 >** Ilex crenata, Rosa, Tillandsia

CHRISTOPHER JAMES
Australia

SŌGETSU

Photography:
Wes Greene

p22 > Doryanthes excelsa   **p133 >** Banksia spinulosa   **p194 >** Acacia pycnantha

LEE JOHNSTONE
Australia

 SŌGETSU

Photography:
David Ryan

p49 > Anemone, Freesia refracta, wild cherry plum blossom

LILY KARMATZ
Australia

 SŌGETSU

Photography:
Lily Karmatz (p63), Chris Osborne (p139)

p63 > Dietes bicolor, Epidendrum, Lomandra longifolia 'Tanita'
p139 > Epidendrum ibaguense, Heliconia, Pygmy date palm (leaves), blossoming branch

CHARLES KINNEAR & ALTA SCOTT
South Africa

 SŌGETSU

Photography:
Kelvin Saunders

p88-89 > Lilium, Sambucus canandensis (Charles & Alta)
p90 > Echevaria, Strelitzia reginae (Charles)
p124 > Cynara scolymus, Gunnera manicata (Alta)

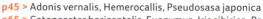

ROSWITHA KLUGE
Germany

IKENOBO

Photography:
Renate & Mathias Tautermann

p45 > Adonis vernalis, Hemerocallis, Pseudosasa japonica
p65 > Cotoneaster horizontalis, Euonymus, Iris sibirica, Paeonia officinalis, Pinus, Pseudosasa, Taxus, Thuja occidentalis
p138 > Acer palmatum, Amaranthus, Chrysanthemum, Cornus sanguine, Ligustrum vulgare, Hydrangea, Pieris japonica, Nephrolepis, Parthenocissus quinquefolia

HELGA KOMAZ
Austria

 SŌGETSU

Photography:
Peter Melbinger

p40 > Tulipa, Viburnum opulus
p41 > Chaenomeles japonica, Spiraea cinerea
p66 > Carex, Helianthus annuus
p108 > Ginkgo biloba, Malus sylvestris

NICOLE KRUIMEL-ROSSELLE
The Netherlands

SŌGETSU

Photography:
Geert de Jong

p46 > Tulipa

LILIANE LABARRIÈRE
(LILIANE LABARRIÈRE, HUGUETTE TRAVERT, ANNE MARIE MOREAU, MICHÈLE BOUTELOUP, SOLANGE LOTTON, MAITE LETOURNEUR)
Germany

SŌGETSU
Photography: Christian Houssard

p180 > Helleborus, moss, red Camellia branches covered with lichen, wood

HELENE LANZ
Germany

SŌGETSU

Photography:
Steffen Dietze

p29 > Magnolia sieboldiana, ceramic container
p171 > Lilium, wood of a beer barrel, iron plate and rod

LISBETH LERUM
Norway

 SŌGETSU

Photography:
Knut Langeland

p191 > Chrysanthemum, Pinus, stones, textiles

CHRISTINA LINDNER
Germany

 SŌGETSU

Photography:
Torsten Krone

p83 > Alchemilla mollis, Hemerocallis, Paeonia
p140-141 > Cydonia oblonga
p157 > Cyclamen

HEDDA LINTNER
Germany

 SŌGETSU

Photography:
Corinna Rogger

p23 > Iris sibirica, Typha
p24 > Petasites hybr., Taraxacum sect. Ruderalia
p106 > Platanus occidentalis, Salix matsudana 'Tortuosa'

ELKE LOHMEYER & UTE GRAVE
Germany

 SŌGETSU

Photography:
Astrid Grave

p25 > Musa textilis (bleached), piece of wood, ostrich egg
p122 > Amaranthus caudatus, Cucurbita, Quercus rubra (leaves)
p123 > Alpinia, Cornus sanguinea, Gleditsia triacanthos
p164 > Edgewortia chrysantha, Zantedeschia aethiopica
p165 > Hydrangea macrophylla, Wisteria floribunda (coloured branch), coloured piece of wood

JO MAINDONALD
Australia

 SŌGETSU

Photography:
David Ryan

p92 > Pyrus ussuriensis

GERDA MATTHEES
Belgium

SŌGETSU

Photography:
Dirk De Greve

p99 > Allium giganteum, Craspedia globosa, palm (leaf)
p100 > Heliconia rostrata

ANKE MA-VERHOEVEN
The Netherlands

 SŌGETSU

Photography:
Fotostudio Zuylenburg

p77 > Rheum rhabarbarum
p184 > Cetraria islandica, Cyclamen, twig with catkins
p185 > Amaryllis, Pyrus communis (twigs)

ERIKA MEIER
Germany

SŌGETSU

Photography:
Gunnar Meier

p73 > Vitis vinifera
p74 > Hydrangea, Physalis franchetti
p175 > Helleborus niger, Pinus

LENIE MERTS
The Netherlands

 SŌGETSU

Photography:
Fotostudio Zuylenburg

p34 > Cacti (dried), Cornus alba, Malus (leaf), Tulipa
p76 > Hosta
p121 > Bergenia, Calamus rotang, Dahlia, Typha
p186 > Lichenes, tree stump
p187 > Bambusa, Betula (bark), Salix (bleached), Sedum

CHINARA MUNDUZBAEVA
Russia

 SŌGETSU

Photography:
Alexey Popov

p42 > Liriope (lily grass), Tulipa
p150 > Aristolochia manshuriensis, Bambusa, Livingstonia (bleached), Pinus

JOAN NORBURY
Australia

 SŌGETSU

Photography:
David Ryan

p177 > Micromyrtus ciliata, Phebalium stenophyllum

WIL OORTMAN-DE THEYE
The Netherlands

SŌGETSU

Photography:
Ton van Etten

p126-127 > Equisetum
p128 > Craspedia globosa
p158 > stainless steel rod, red plastic rod, plastic plates

DENISE PRIEM-WILLEMARCK
Belgium

 SŌGETSU

Photography:
Denise Priem-Willemarck

p137 > Asparagus plumosus, Celastrus orbiculatus, Cocos nucifera (dried)

JEANNE RAUWENHOFF
The Netherlands

ICHIYO

Photography:
Hette Koopmans

p81 > Gleichenia polypodioides, Rosa felicia 'Pink Nevada'
p134 > Bergenia, Hydrangea macrophylla, Wisteria

ADRIENNE SARTORI
Australia

 SŌGETSU

Photography:
David Ryan

p71 > Iris, Phormium tenax

THEA SARTORI
Australia

SŌGETSU

Photography:
David Ryan

p48 > Viburnum tinus, Wisteria sinensis

HENRIËTTE SCHALK
The Netherlands

 SŌGETSU

Photography:
Monique van de Ven

p84 > Anemone coronaria, Wisteria
p131 > Carpinus betulis, Rosa 'Bonica' (rosebuds)
p174 > Wisteria, kindling

JENNEKE SOEJOKO-OOSTERVELD
The Netherlands

 SŌGETSU

Photography:
Ruud van Stralen

p50 > Hyacinthus orientalis
p51 > Euphorbia fulgens, Hyacinthus orientalis, Sanseveria trifasciata
p154 > Pinus, Palm (bleached)

BARBARA SOLNORDAL
Australia

SŌGETSU

Photography:
David Ryan

p176 > Limonium, Phoenix dactilifera

ELS SPOELSTRA-GOOS
The Netherlands

 SŌGETSU

Photography:
Ton van Etten

p35 > Crambe, Hyacinthus, Typha **p36 >** Anthurium, Magnolia, Morus, Spiraea
p75 > Anthurium, Equisetum **p110 >** Allium, Asplenium nidus, Catalpa
p160 > Betula, Cryptomeria, Phalaenopsis **p161 >** Euonymus, Lunaria annua
p162 > Avena

MONIQUE VAN DE VEN
The Netherlands

 SŌGETSU

Photography:
Monique van de Ven

p54 > Corylus avellana 'Contorta', Raku ceramics by Monique van de Ven
p55 > Bambusa, Muscari latifolium, ceramics by Monique van de Ven
p56 > Bambusa, Ceramics by Monique van de Ven
p192 > Corylus avellana 'Contorta', silicone glue

GODELIEVE VAN DEN HEUVEL –
JANSSENS
Belgium

 OHARA

Photography:
Peter Staes

p19 > Iris pseudocarus, Magnolia kobus, Spiraea **p20-21 >** Chamaecyparis pisifera 'Squarrosa', Forsythia giraldiana, Narcissus 'Tête à Tête', Sticherus cunninghamii (umbrella fern) **p82 >** Acornus callamus variegatus, Asarum caudatum, Darmera peltata, Lysimachia punctata, Sasaella glabra abostriata **p104 >** Brunera variegata, Malus, Vicia cracca **p105 >** Aster fricartii, Chrysanthemum indicum hybr 'Shoesmith', Photergilla **p148 >** Kalanchoë, Mandina domestica, Pinus parviflora **p149 >** Chamaecyparis squarrosa, Leucothoë, Pinus sylvestris, Skimmia

CORRIE VAN DER MEER -
FISCHER
The Netherlands

 ICHIYO

Photography:
Hette Koopmans

p168-169 > Cedrus, Eucharis, Prunus spinosa

ROBERT VAN HECKE
Belgium

 SŌGETSU

Photography:
Annika Ingelaere

p85 > Anemone, Yucca
p143 > Aspidistra, Citrus sinensis

KARINE VAN NYEN
Belgium

 IKENOBO

Photography:
Karine Van Nyen

p37 > Chaenomeles, Chrysanthemum, Camellia, Ilex, Iris, Prunus, Skimmia
p103 > Chrysanthemum, Iris, Spirea salicifolia

THÉRÈSE VAN OVERSTYNS
Belgium

OHARA

Photography:
J-P Van der Elst

p31 > Arum italicum 'Marmoratum', Chrysanthemum 'Roblush',
Corylus avellana 'Contorta'

DESIREE VAN VLIET
The Netherlands

 SŌGETSU

Photography:
Fotostudio Zuylenburg

p80 > Hibiscus, Iris (leaf)

JEANNINE VANHEE-CORDEEL
Belgium

SŌGETSU

Photography:
Philippe Leyssens

p16-17 > Spiraea, Ranunculus, Rhododendron vaseyi
p18 > Spiraea, Tulipa, Typha

MARJA VERVOORT-BIEMOND
The Netherlands

SŌGETSU

Photography:
Jan Pieter Roggeveen

p62 > Helianthus annuus
p116 > Euonymus
p151 > Catalpa, Fagus sylvatica

ULRIKE VOGLER
Germany

SŌGETSU

Photography:
Hans-Peter Vogler

p129 > Brunia leavis, Leucospermum nutans, Leucadendron 'Kameleon',
Vitis juniperus

MARIAN VOORHOEVE-OLDEMAN
The Netherlands

 SŌGETSU

Photography:
Fotostudio Zuylenburg

p120 > Gypsophila, Miscanthus, Rosa (hips)

MARCEL VRIGNAUD
France

OHARA

Photography:
Marcel Vrignaud

p30 > Acer platanoïdes, Iris germanica, Wisteria floribunda
p87 > Iris pseudo-acorus (leaves), Nelumbo nucifera (leaves, flower and seed pod),
Saggitaria latifolia (leaves), Scirpus lacustris (leaves)
p135 > Lilium, Lonicera, Viburnum opulus, dried mushroom

ANNE RIET VUGTS-LUYTEN
The Netherlands

 SŌGETSU

Photography:
Ton van Etten

p12 > Narcissus 'Cheerfulness', Salix babylonica
p132 > Acer platanoides 'Crimson King'
p155 > Betula (schors), Pinus mugo, Phalaenopsis 'Red Lips'
p156 > Callicarpa bodinieri, Ilex crenata convexa

URSULA WEHR
Germany

 SŌGETSU

Photography:
Angelika Raatz

p190 > Fagus sylvatica, felt ball

MARGARET WILSON
Australia

 SŌGETSU

Photography:
David Ryan

p70 > Rosa 'White Wings', Stipa gigantea

URSULA WINAND
Germany

 SOGETSU
IKENOBO

Photography:
Werner Möhler

p43 > Prunus, Ranunculus, Ruscus p45 > Alchemilla, Curcuma, Typha
p67 > Asplenium, Gloriosa, Typha p68 > Allium, Calla, Iris
p101 > Nandina, Helianthus, Iris p102 > Anthurium, Cornus, Phormium, Physalis,
Xanthorrhoea p195 > Euphorbia spinosa, Gypsophila, angel hair

MITZI YAU
Canada

 OHARA

Photography:
Simon Tsang

p125 > Brassica oleraceae convar. acephala, Corylus avellana 'Contorta', kale

OLGA YUDINA
Russia

 SŌGETSU

Photography:
Alexey Popov

p27 > Hydrangea macrophylla, Ricinus p28 > Narcissus, Syringa vulgaris
Cover / p113 > Physalis, Pinus (bark) p114 > Haloxylon, Pinus (bark), Sorbus
aucuparia p115 > Triticum, Pinus p166 > Capsicum annuum, Pinus
p167 > Acer (leaf), Pinus

URSULA ZEMBROT
Germany

 SŌGETSU

Photography:
Gunnar Meier

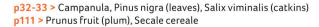

p32-33 > Campanula, Pinus nigra (leaves), Salix viminalis (catkins)
p111 > Prunus fruit (plum), Secale cereale

GABY ZÖLLNER-GLUTSCH
Germany

SHIN EIGETSU SHOFU RYU

Photography:
Bernhard Müller

p130 > Cucurbita (hokkaido)

Previously published

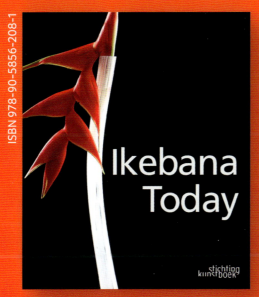

ISBN 978-90-5856-208-1

Ikebana Today
sold out!

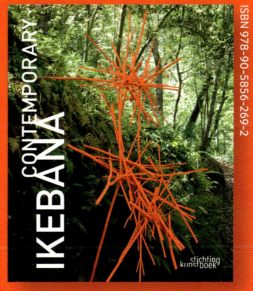

ISBN 978-90-5856-269-2

Contemporary Ikebana
€59.90

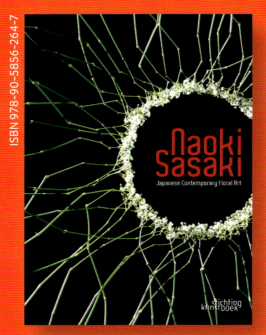

ISBN 978-90-5856-264-7

Naoki Sasaki
Japanese Contemporary Floral Art
€39.90

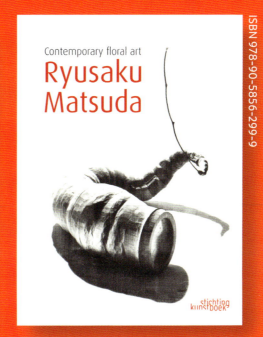

ISBN 978-90-5856-299-9

Ryusaku Matsuda
Contemporary Floral Art
€39.90

Ikebana
through all seasons

Introduction & coordination
Mit Ingelaere-Brandt

Final editing
Katrien Van Moerbeke

Layout
www.groupvandamme.eu

Print
www.pureprint.be

Published by
Stichting Kunstboek bvba
Legeweg 165
B-8020 Oostkamp
Belgium
Tel. +32 50 46 19 10
Fax +32 50 46 19 18
info@stichtingkunstboek.com
www.stichtingkunstboek.com

ISBN 978-90-5856-367-5
D/2011/6407/04
NUR 421